We're All
Mad Here

by Claudia Turner

For my daughter Dakota, who inspires me to get off my butt and write every day. I love you.

Contents

5

6

7

"But I don't want to go among mad people,"

Alice remarked.

"Oh, you can't help that," said the Cat: "We're all mad here.

I'm mad. You're mad."

—Lewis Carroll, *Alice in Wonderland*

I

We're All Mad Here

It was between this and that,
and I chose this, and that
has made all the difference.

Some people say to fight for what you want.
I say, why fight for the idiot who didn't treasure you in the first place?
Fight a better fight.
Don't fight at all.
Stop holding on to the one who got away so more can get away,
and you wonder why you're all alone chasing your bucket list in this discount hotel sharing sourdough with your dog.
Why not just say "no"?
You don't have to explain why, you're not the president or an OSHA inspector.
Drive to the redwoods and camp under a canopy of aerial netted suspension bridges attached like parasites to 3,000-year-old trees.
You hate feeling attached. You hate feeling tied down.
That's why you're floating away in a cloud of balloons.

We're all mad here.
A plague of fools and dreamers,
anonymous lovers in photographs.
One day at a time. One bar at a time.
A cigarette for overactive minds.
Play hard to get, play easy, get lost, get engaged.
It will go away, this infinite sadness,
this bottomless pit of desperate connections.
Grow up and get it together.
Too emotional, too romantic, too many feels.
Feelings are out; real estate is in;
yoga retreats to Bali, life and wealth mastery workshops;
good credit, IRA's,
savings for a down payment on an electric car.
Save feelings for theaters, therapists,
trips to Europe where you run into an expat and fuck.
Sometimes even practical people need a good fuck.

You can't write down your heart.
But if you want to deconstruct it,
purée some nerves and unconscious pornography.
Get quiet, breathe and listen to
the words floating through your body.
Make sure they're your own and not your mother's.
Go for a drive,
put the words on a napkin,
let the garbage out to make room for the roots.
Start with a laugh.
Let yourself cry.
Write their name again and again.
Write around their name. Erase their name.
Their name is Everyone.

Everyone's paying off student loans and
buying stocks and accumulating mortgages,
social security, savings, 401Ks like
they're going to live to old age.
What's that even?
200 years ago it was my age.
And like that curly-haired psycho in Ozark says:
I don't know shit about fuck.

Sorry lonely, depressed men,
I'm not a therapy hotline or
emotional trashcan.
Sorry, you're going to have to drive around me,
I'm taking pictures of rusty bathtubs in cow fields.
Sorry I had feelings,
I'll replace them with jokes right away.
I once bought a book called "How To Be
Interesting" and never opened it. Sorry.
Sorry I'm on edge and I cut you in half,
but my ego is fragile and you are hurting it.
I'm sorry, you were a flower,
and I pulled off all your petals.
I'm sorry I told you I liked you,
that was stupid and will never happen again.
I'm sorry I scare you but I think it's because you like me.
I'm sorry about all the sorries,
I recommend reading them with a little
soft jazz to lighten the mood.

Tired of sounding like a jilted lover? Middle-aged loafer?
Press a narrative compliment on a stranger with aggressive
smiles,
Honk desperate boredom on warm gusts of wind,
Shout a staccato of essays at well-bred exchange students.
Scream in capitalist, indifferent shrugs.
Create boundaries with your Queen of Hearts father.
Create boundaries with your Mock Turtle mother.
Wake listless colleagues with arm punches.
Pick up whispers from dry mouths in service entrances.
Straighten heavy coat sleeves and parade through dark alleys.
Drive off-ramp on a street of industrial piss-stained art.
Make hollowed-out holes to pour feelings out.
Repeat.

Drop dead,
not bombs.
You told me to really be
enlightened I had to leave the world I knew—
gossip girls, house parties, poker
nights, 80's nights, Taco nights—
Drop dead to live.
Drop dead and become a ghost.
Live in this apartment, sit on this lap,
Forever and ever.
You were the father I never had.
I was the doll you always wanted.
The sun will shine on my kneecaps forever.
The smell of rice and saffron.

In Portland— after a year abroad, teaching English in Asia,
and backpacking third-world countries like a Hemingway
impersonator— I was broke.
Young, restless, addicted to coffee.
Skinny jeans, big glasses.
I was Portland.
Half of us unemployed,
typing memoirs about nothingness in
gluten-free, organic cafes,
listening to Bob Dylan, getting high in the alley.
I saw a child disappear and an old man die,
a rotting hermit in front of his TV.
Everything was finite, intangible, exhausting.
A crumb in my pocket and a crumb on the window.
A crumb the child left behind.
In the end we're all fertilizer for flowers.
"Cloudy you're such a sweetheart
when you aren't needy and full of expectations."
I scattered the flames into smaller,
manageable corners, and smothered them with hope and
melatonin. I was disappointed and speechless,
staring through a void of white walls and IKEA,
sipping dark roast and oat milk,
wondering how I could wonder so damn much.
Things didn't always need explaining.
Things just happened.
I happened to things, and things happened to me,
and things happened to things.
Things happened and happened all the goddamn time.
I decided to move.
If I couldn't get him out of my heart
I'd pry him out of my head, and move east.
"You'll never meet anyone like me," Adam said,
more offended than heartbroken.
We were panting and smoking cigarettes
after what was clearly our last fuck.
He had this idea we'd meet every few years
in a cabin somewhere,

and fuck again for old times' sake,
but I knew better.

———

The Guatemalan moon looked like a giant ingrown toenail.
We drove the wrong direction on a flooded road
winding through the hills.
"Cloudy is a cloud on a blank canvas," John said.
The paranoid driver Dwight's keys were lost
and now John wanted his sister to move 100s of quetzales,
about 200 less, from Bank of America,
to a local bank, to Wayne.
Who's Wayne?
Everyone was lying.
Chaos.
Dwight was in charge of the American Embassy.
Everyone had a story and a rumor.
Dwight had to drive his kid to school,
left his youngest at home,
trashed his crazy wife.
Chaos in every country.

———

From Guatemala to New York,
straight from JFK to Clifton, New Jersey.
A couple of Chinese businessmen making MSG-laden bulk
soy for all the Whole Foods hot bars from New York to
Massachusetts. I'd give my "Creative Director" ideas and
they'd say no, and I'd say no. Fucking businessmen.
Snake oil salesmen of post-industrial society.
We drove to the Whole Foods NE Headquarters and
stores in Manhattan and Boston. This was pre-Bezos.
We shelled out soy samples to boho shoppers who made
Carrie Bradshaw look like a poser. When I suggested a new

logo or social media idea John groaned.
I wasn't creatively directing shit.
I was a pawn, not a New Yorker, a west coast transient, a
Jersey squatter, a rootless nomad.
The bus pulled up in front of the New York Times building.
I walked out into a swarm of bees—
tall bees, fat bees, loud, abrasive bees.
Lady Gaga finally made sense.
"I'm on the right track baby, I was BORN THIS WAY."
All the clutter in my reflective mind poured out
to the giant urban symphony around me and I was submerged,
bridging the gap between my interior and exterior worlds.
Starbucks and hot dog stands on every corner,
terriers on leashes, and accents, hundreds of accents.
I walked. For hours I walked.
Simone de Beauvoir said, "There is something in the New
York air that makes sleep useless." If I'd pursued molecular
physics, maybe I'd have said it was the energy from so many
top-notch atoms floating in one magnificent space.
The MET smelled like perfume, mothballs, money,
crème brûlée.
Hours past Duchamp and Van Gogh and Dior evening gowns,
like an extra in my own movie. I knew it wouldn't last.
The breeze from the Hudson, Liberty a blurry smudge, the
MOMA, the MET, the hair, the plaid, old cathedrals and
young skyscrapers disappearing into the clouds;
cute taxi bikers, toddlers in Central Park taking Pilates,
girls in mini-skirts with big, horn-rimmed glasses,
stilettos, short and tall, fat and thin,
Portuguese, French, German, Japanese,
Radio City Music Hall, Rockefeller Center,
break dancers on 5th Avenue, tarot readers on Crosby.
Sunset down 42nd St., between Broadway and neon lights,
Coronas in the subway, all-nighters in the park with an old
friend who also liked walking in the middle of the street and
probably liked me but I never could see past my own broken
heart. One night, after dinner in Manhattan with my
roommate, we walked past a crowd of pedestrians, firefighters,

police officers.
"What the hell is this?"
Nudging closer, we saw the body.
Someone had just jumped off the roof of the building adjacent
to our restaurant.
"Have you ever seen someone die like that?"
"Kind of," I said, full, and nauseous, and tongue-tied.
Life was fleeting, nonsensical, painful, random,
It was everywhere here, revolting, glorious, and raw.
I was young and ready to live it.
The melting pot dripping off me—
the smells, the smiles, the colors, the noises.
I felt my shell crack open.

"Spooky action at a distance."

—*Albert Einstein*

II

Quantum Entanglement

I wanted to haunt your bed every night,
when you couldn't sleep,
and every little noise pierced your ears.
You're a great magician,
hiding your feelings like that.
Focused on the invisible list.
Everyone and their list.
Your eyes shined when you forgot about it.
Focused on my neck.
I saw you seeing me,
the force that sustains the Universe,
the intent.
We're all dying, and
this moment is dead before it has ended.
Another vacuum in time and space,
another look,
a history of looks,
a vaguely frustrating jealousy,
and then space.
Lots of space.
All the space.
The last gasp of space.
The end.

You said you wanted a weird girl,
but when you got me,
you didn't want me anymore.
I guess you wanted a marketable weird,
like a Northern Exposure weird,
with a pixie haircut and those tiny bangs
that skim the forehead like pubes.
I guess you wanted the kind of weird you can take home
to mama and say "look ma, I found a girl with the same
haircut
as you. Are you happy now?"

Brain: I don't know much but I have a Master's degree to prove it.

[montage of me trying to decide what socks bring me joy after watching "Tidying Up With Marie Kondo"]

Lady: "Excuse me, where's a good place to eat around here?"

Me: "Sorry, I was an English major."

[montage like that scene in Good Will Hunting where Will is furiously scribbling math equations but it's me drawing dicks around literary quotes]

Body: Go to bed.

Brain: Harrison Ford was Joan Didion's carpenter.

Body: Go to bed.

Brain: A person who will die tomorrow is currently drinking beer and thinking about a TV show, isn't that weird?

I dissected your laugh and found question marks,
liquor, T.S. Eliot,
Rilke, Rimbaud,
questions, indigestion, allergies,
rebellion, establishment,
anger, hope,
failure, humiliation,
Flaubert,
the American Revolution,
the French Revolution,
masturbation,
one-night stands turned into miserable relationships,
Victorian literature,
nature documentaries,
The Velvet Underground,
ping-pong, Hollywood,
humanitarianism, student loans,
Alice in Wonderland, platonic blow jobs,
unrequited love, old photographs,
half-written letters, rain, cold baths,
sleepless nights, sunrise, rug burn,
soft breathing, gasps,
disassociation through vanilla ice cream and
Godard films,
Kurosawa,
2 am with internal critics, *tap tap tap*ping
on the countertop,
tap tap tap

I'd been watching Goodfellas.
Billy Batts was getting beaten to death
on the floor of the bar,
Donovan played in the background,
Sandra leaned on the counter,
"Did ya make the drawings on the wall?"
"Huh? Ya" I said, one eye on Billy,
one eye on Sandra.
My mouth was hot.
My feet were cold.
I was microwaving lavender aromatherapy
slippers from the hospital gift shop.
My feet were swollen like a cantaloupe.
My tummy was swollen like a watermelon.
"I heard you asked for a Bible."
"I did?"
"That's what I heard."
"Oh no, I didn't do that."
She stood next to my bed and stared down at me.
"Who said that?"
"I don't know." Squinting.
She finally gave me a pity smile and left.
"Bitch," I mumbled, grabbing the phone by the bed.
I called my Nana.
"HELLO?"
"HOW ARE YOU?"
"YOUR MOM IS AT THE FAIR."
"NO, YOU, I WANT TO TALK TO YOU.
HOW ARE YOU?"
She hung up. My favorite old person.
My favorite person.
Old, deaf, no teeth, 96, getting shorter daily,
her hair was still golden and soft,
I missed her.

———

I walked to the gift shop.
They had a sale on pocket charms.
"WHEN ARE YOU DUE?"
A gray-haired lady was frowning at me.
"Why?"
"Because— I wanted to know."
"October" I shuffled away.
No smile. Nothing.
Staring at my tummy like an art installation.
"Bitch" I muttered, waddling away.
My water broke. Fluid. Blood.
My heart was going to explode.
"Breathe."
Blood pressure in the 180-s.
"We're going to surgery."
"I don't want that."
"We have to."
"No."
"Sorry."
"There must be some kind of way out of here…"
Hendrix and bright lights and
my stomach split open but I couldn't feel.
Something cool.
"I can't get no relief…"
A blue cover in my face.
"I want to see."
"Sorry."
Ok, I'm ok, this is my fucking life.
Soft movement in the far distance.
A kick? A cry?
A pink body. Tiny.
Chubby cheeks. A cry.
Shaking and magnesium.
A tiny body on my naked, stitched belly.
This is our fucking life.
In the morning I got a call.
Nana had died.
The bed was still warm.

37

"What you see before you, my friend, is the result of a lifetime of chocolate."

—Katharine Hepburn

III

Eat Me Like One of Your
French Pastries

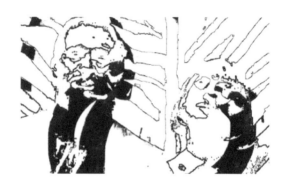

I don't know how to categorize my emotions
now that mix tapes are no longer a thing.
Making a guy buy a Spotify membership just to listen to my
playlist is why our planet is nearing its 6th mass extinction.
Too many know-it-alls, not enough knowing.
Adults are just big children with invisible baggage
they hit you in the head with
when you're not looking.
But it's fine.
If you're feeling down, just pretend
you're an FBI agent undercover.
I'll take you to a remote Wyoming ghost town where we can
learn survival skills like how to integrate our shadows and
reparent our inner Kevin Arnolds.
If it's very quiet we might hear the sound of our hearts and
heads whispering to each other.

I wonder what my dogs think
about when I'm playing historical dramas
with Medieval music.
I wonder what my cat is thinking about
when she sits curled up at my feet staring
at me for hours and sharpening
her Hattori Hanzo sword.
I wonder if my dogs and cat think they're going
to live forever or realize they got the
short-end of the stick.

Eat me like one of
your French pastries.
I'll take you to a dive bar
in the middle of the woods
and we'll wander around
'til a ghost eats us.
You, me, and a
bottle of Arsenic.

I'm always on the verge of running 3 miles or
drinking a bottle of wine.
Depression's the only diet I've ever been on,
but it sure does work.
My fashion sense is Lumberjack meets ballet dancer.
My modus operandi amor is Socrates at an orgy.
My creepy level, on a scale of cute golden retriever puppy to
monster-clawed Stephen King IT clown, is eyeless doll head.
Some days I want to be an international investigative reporter
in Paris; other days I want to watch Netflix.
My twin flame probably married a communications major
with fake boobs 20 years ago and has ten kids.
My entire life is a dust particle.
I'm not saying I want to be Amish but I wouldn't mind a horse
and carriage, and a cute hat.
I just need to find a kind, compassionate guy
who hates people as much as I do.
We'll meet at a codependents anonymous meeting and
become independent together.
We'll peel off the layers to see if
our cores match.
If the conversation gets too serious,
we'll take our pants off.
And when spring returns,
we'll go tell it on the mountain.

Between single-photon quantum
memory diamond and slow cooker
tapioca pudding, how does your
brain feel today?
All your lonely moments
transformed into raindrops,
showering down on your sleeping
body until you're drowning
in one giant blue
memory ocean.

What do you want to be
when you blow up?
I want to be stardust,
atoms and synthetic
diamonds.
I hope we're a cluster of
atoms floating around in the
same endless expanse
of space together
one day,
and when the
atmosphere and oceans
evaporate into space,
the Sun expands
beyond Earth's
orbit,
and all life is vaporized,
you will still be with me.

I'm sorry to raise this
controversial subject
on Valentine's Day,
but the Bachelor
seems to discriminate
against
short-haired ladies,
and I believe
that's at
the root
of each couple's
eventual demise.

I stayed silent because they said,
Silence is where you find answers,
and when enough time had passed feeling the sun on my head,
in a dream, I was back in Portland, on a park bench.
A white light gave me a hug,
and I opened a door between trees,
walked down steps to my body below,
where I stepped into a giant black hole.
And there I opened my eyes and felt
more awake than I had in days.
The light whispered in my ear,
Remember when your dad would be late
and your mom would wander around impatiently
getting more lost looking for him?
"Yes" I said, scratching my ear. "She couldn't just sit the fuck
down and wait."
For you to find what you seek,
stand still, or sit on this bench, and feel everything...
don't act until it's no longer a reaction...
let go of the pain and rage and clenching inside you
so you can recognize love.
It won't go anywhere, even if your 3D reality sees other
obstacles, people,
struggles in your way.
The real thing won't go anywhere, it just needs to be seen.
It's there waiting for you to see it.
And I asked "What about *him*? My person? Where is *he*?"
He's on the mountain with you...on the same path.
And I stayed silent because everything I wanted to say felt
meaningless, and as the sun felt warm on my head like a
cerebral fondue, melting memories into soup, they said,
Silence is where you find answers,
and when enough time had passed feeling the sun...

Anger is alive.
Peace is an art.

When my head's not exploding into a million pieces,
I'm a sweet girl.
A thoughtful and tender girl.
I like cake, jokes, Paris, theatre, trees, rocks, space.
The day before yesterday,
standing in a corner where the light was dim,
I heard a breath and heavy beats.
The dark mass of a cloud and explosion.
The quiet joy in deep release,
a million visions, a cave of stalactite,
a cemetery, a glance,
an outstretched leg, a glass of wine,
a smile, a room,
a bed, an endless sea.
The heavy beats were my heart
in your head, or your head in my heart.
BOOM. BOOM.
The breath was my breath in your mouth.
The explosion was my body with your body.
What a mad idea I have acting it all out
before it's happened.
Nobody can understand this feeling,
covered up and living heavy in my gut.

(I wrote this before it happened,
and when it happened you were triggered
because you had a panic attack.
We were so close. We were a volcano.
Let's do it again.)

My sex tape is just a series
of sensual songs I recorded
off the radio in high school.
I like to strut around my apartment
with a towel on my head
like the 19th-century Rebel Queen,
Maharani Jindan Kaur.
Tonight I'm in a towel nibbling
a tangerine in bed with
my legs propped on a giant
elephant if you were wondering
if I'm sexy or not.
Maybe you should get
on top of me. Press me
into the mattress
like a flower in a book.

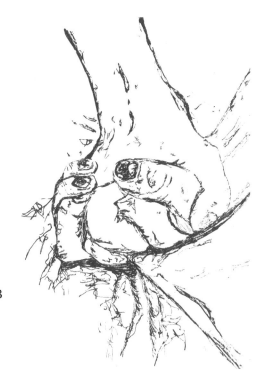

53

Lucky raindrops get to touch your face.
I like your eyes.
Did they come from your mom or dad?
What's your middle name?
Do you smell like a forest?
Can I lick your face?

A hug is a gateway drug to a kiss.
I need a hug.
Thinking of making some money at the
local farmer's market this summer by
selling some fermented, sustainable, organic,
mystical, sacred, grass-fed, non-GMO
hugs, but no kisses.
Those I'm saving for you.
gets nervous about stuff
I just want a fuck buddy who is
monogamous, wants to cuddle,
thinks I'm amazing, and loves me
just the way I am, is that
so much to ask?
I'd probably just lay in bed and
cuddle all day if that was an option.
Start with a hug or two or five.
In another time and place
you and I are spooning and also
you rub my feet and also
I suck your dick and we're happy.
Spooning and fucking. Maybe next week?
When you wish upon a star, the
star is already dead and so is your wish.
Never mind, I'm just sad.
All this waiting is giving me road rage.

I was pretending to read a book.
A loud cover, yellow I think,
faded yellow like a morning sunrise or smoker's teeth.
I'd ruined another possibility,
tried too hard, showed too many feelings.
Now to rest. Hold a book in a park.
Stare at it like a meteor shower.
I would have pulled out a Nat Sherman ten years ago,
the fantasia colored pack, with gold, charcoal filters.
Now I take a deep breath.
A string of breaths.
My body pressed against dirt and tree.
Heavy and light.

I miss traveling.
I miss lukewarm crap coffee on
a train to a place I've never been.
Sometimes I make coffee at
home while I'm getting ready to
drive to town for coffee.
I try to do all my town chores
on Sunday morning when
it's just me and the other
sinners on the street.
Do you ever wonder what
your life would have been
like if you were a
morning person?

I was thinking about how I once sent
you a letter and some art and gave
you the wrong last name on the
front of the envelope: Owen. Fucking Owen.
And you said, maybe I'd associated
you with Luke Wilson because "Matthew Mark
Luke and John" and Texas and your son Wilson
and brother Owen or something like that.
Anyway. However you said it, I liked you
right then even more than I had when I first
saw you talking on a banana.
The Super Bowl was last night
so while most people were out drinking and gathering
and tweeting about L.A. and Ohio and balls
and half-times, I was at home in my pajamas
trying to think up what I'd say to you if tomorrow (today)
(on this vacuous holiday named after a pagan festival
and stoned/beheaded saint), I
could gather the nerve to send you
a few words.
I thought maybe I could tell
you a joke: "Terrifying if literal:
my feet are killing me."
Or I could be super serious: "Are you ever
Trying to put on your pants while
standing but your feet keep getting stuck
in the middle of the pants? Life
feels like that a lot."
Or romantic: "Lucky raindrops
get to touch your face."
But I figured if you're really an
INTP, none of those lines would play out
well and I should just keep it simple, scientific
and honest: "We're all star stuff, connected
biologically and anatomically in our
shared journey through this vast Universe,
and I like your star stuff."

History is quick and the ghosts return.
Gold-plated shit and basements
with retro furniture.
Too many comedians in tracksuits.
Is everyone at the same party?
It's getting crowded in here.
Everyone knows everyone,
and everyone's a stranger.
Put your trash in a bag and throw it
in a storage unit.
Everyone's eyes tell a story.
Even if they forget the
trauma and mythology.
I wonder about your eyes.
Are they still gray, green, blue?
I buy flowers to forget.

Why was I drawn to you?
Your sharp eyes.
Your soft smirk.
Your Eddie Vedder hair.
Your rosy beige Lebowski bathrobe.
Your stupid confidence.
Your face.
Stuck in my head.
Again.
I don't know.
You're not doing well, stuck there, in my head.
Stagnant.
A corpse.
Silent for once.
I just wanted to know why.
Was I your gift? Your trash?
We were soulmates, so wrong in retrospect.
If we hadn't worked together or lived in the same complex
I'd have never looked twice.
Convenience is a bitch.
The time in the hallway,
were you waiting for me?
Spatula in hand, baking brownies,
I was ready to serve, down on my knees.
Obedient. That didn't last long.
The sex was something.
Were you thinking of her when I thought about him?
Didn't think I'd miss you so bad,
it was never love, but I still couldn't cut you out of my head.
So awkward to think about how much time I lost.

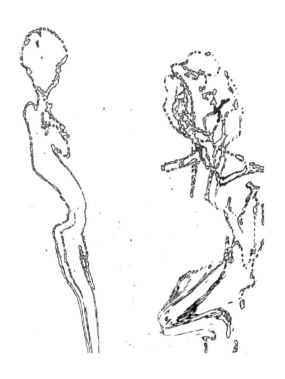

Conversations while dating myself:
Me: You're making me nervous.
Me: Doesn't everything make you nervous?
Me: So what.
Me: Do you want to get ice cream?
Me: I'd love to.
Me: Here, let me get the door.
Me: Oh, thank you.
Me: You look stunning.
Me: [blush] Stop it.
Me: Why're you so weird?
Me: I just want someone who loves me unconditionally.
Me: It's your day off—ready to do something fun?
Me: No.
Me: You worry too much.
Me: No I don't. Why do you say that? What—
Me: I've never been on a hot-air balloon.
Me: What—
Me: My feet smell like pineapple, here, smell.
Me: It's hurting my feelings.
Me: What?
Me: Everything.
Me: I like you.
Me: Oh yeah?
Me: Never mind. I don't like you. I never liked you.
Me: Shut up.
Me: Tell me I'm pretty.
Me: Like how?
Me: Like "I'd fuck you."
Me: I'd fuck you.
Me: [blush] Stop it.

"Life changes fast. Life changes in the instant. You sit down to dinner and life as you know it ends."

—Joan Didion

IV

The Only Thing Left in 100 Years Will Be Love

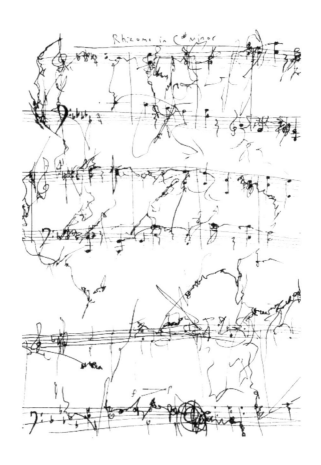

A year before D&D was invented,
a boy was born in Dallas, Texas.
He grew up there in Cowboy land,
dated a witch, played in a band.
He went off to college, up north in Boston,
traveled, smoked, drank and read often.
He opened his heart, again and again,
'til finally his heart had grown quite thin.
It stretched and it popped out of his chest.
Vulnerable in love, he felt a hot mess.
'Til one last girl, a whippoorwill dream,
left him rundown, all out of steam.
He'd torn down his walls and let her in,
just to get sick, and shed his thick skin.
When it finally ended, he felt like a stranger,
a dead man walking, in constant danger.
He built up more walls, found a routine,
got a new house, new car, new degree.
But the walls he had built, that made him feel strong,
also made it hard to be real, to move on.
There was always this space between him and another,
even sometimes with his own mother.
Wondering what was the root cause of his problems,
and how, why, or when he'd finally solve them,
he met a new girl he kind of fancied,
who talked kind of weird, and seemed to like dancing.
They both had trauma, wounds from the past,
the same quirks and dreams, a taste for high class.
He was attracted to her, but also repelled,
like too much touching would make him spelled.
What did it mean? Was his heart sick?
Was it a sign to ghost this strange chick?
His confusion stemmed from the hard fact
that when he found love he'd soon after crack.
Life sucked sometimes, of this he was certain,
loved ones would leave, hearts would get broken.
This girl he fancied, fancied him too,
she knew his soul, and felt its deep blue,

she knew she liked him, her atoms would dance,
when he was close, they'd fall in a trance.
She wanted more, a few walls removed,
from the Dallas boy with a thing for the blues.
Her Easy Bake Oven, her strange flying ace,
a poet, a father, a real basket-case.
Imperfectly perfect, a man of the world,
a sexy daddy, a heart of gold.
She had no expectations, no great demands,
she just missed his voice, his eyes, his warm hands.
This life is short, we age and scrape by,
sometimes we open up, sometimes we hide.
Sometimes we love, and sometimes abide,
we're only getting older, and soon we will die.
She wanted to know him, the walls removed,
the boy from Dallas with a thing for the blues.
But he closed the gates, swallowed the key,
raised the drawbridge, jumped in the sea.
Always a stranger, no longer a friend,
briefly a lover, a ghost again.

Love after trauma is a chess game with checkers.
That's why I touch all the trees on my path.
I envy their roots, their rhizome communion.
Gods of the forest weaving through dirt,
and reminding us to slow down and convert
all our shit into wisdom.
What a shady century to be in love.
Love's a plague,
wear masks 'til it goes away.
Love needs to be reinvented, Rimbaud said,
but we cling to pawns wishing for kings.
When we die to the world, we're reborn in flowers.
But here we live, our heads in the sand.
Things that have ended endlessly are ending again.

Shed fear,
shed ghosts,
shed sorrow,
shed lists for ideal lovers,
they'll never match the
perfectly imperfect thing
you never knew you needed,
by summer you'll feel it,
by winter you'll see it,
and so it goes.

He handed me a lemon drop with a little too much vodka
"don't let the existential dread set in…not yet"
we were Paul Newman and Geraldine Page in Sweet Bird of
Youth, cigarettes hanging from the corners of our mouths,
sometimes we would share one and
it was almost as good as a kiss
"let's go to the bar"
"the Pythagoreans kept knowledge of the dodecahedron secret
from the public…"
"yeah but old porn weirds me out because you know those
people are slathering wrinkle cream and crocheting mittens
now"
"…and when Hippasus showed the public the sacred shape, he
was drowned…"
"wrinkle cream and viagra…drink"
"so the dodecahedron is a representation of hidden and
protected knowledge"
"you have the most beautiful chin"
"thanks"
life was strange with this vodka and this chessboard and our
language only we could follow and these dodecahedrons and
cigarettes and all the living organisms around us
just working on fucking and survival,
sure I thought about that too,
but I couldn't ruin this beautiful friendship,
this meandering conversation, this tension…
summer ended and we dispersed
come to Spain, you can drink between classes here…
and smoke at the hair salon,
and play piano at the Irish pub…
I miss you…
come see the Goya exhibit, and Dali in Catalonia
y tu puedes practicar español conmigo?

———

73

(hope you miss me)
te echo de menos...
and the term ended and a new one started and Spain faded and
there you were again,
not mine, never mine, but still there, touching distance,
I could smell you,
I could taste you on the cigarette between my lips...
"what was your earliest childhood memory?"
"I was on a cold tile floor surrounded by moving boxes"
"were you lonely?"
"I don't know...seems like it"
"remember when you were a kid and said I TRIPLE DOG
DARE YOU TIMES INFINITY and your friend would say I
QUADRUPLE DOG DARE YOU TIMES INFINITY PLUS
ONE?"
"like it was yesterday"
"good thing time is an illusion"
"a social construct"
"we're practically still playing four square"
"and red rover"
"and duck duck goose"
"and freeze tag"
"and hopscotch"
"and bloody murder"
"I fucking miss four square"
"infinity is implicitly understood until it is described"
"drink"

If the gaze of the other is
a reflection of my inner state,
you are the distinguished truth
behind the androgynous shapeless
children in my mind.
Sitting in a hotel room
of subjunctives and foggy windows,
you consult memories and words.
You sit and wait, wait and sit,
and get old and mad, mad and old.

I bought another expensive device.
It did not cure my trauma.
Hypnosis for trauma works better in YouTube videos.
Virtual-reality. Flooding. EMDR. Somatic experiencing.
Happy Baby. Downward dog.
Rummaging through the attic to jump-start an old filter in 3 Acts.
Dead.
Wobbly.
Blinking awake.

Walking through the produce aisle
I saw a man holding broccoli like a baby and
I thought about when you held me,
and I wanted to buy broccoli
and make tea with it and
drink it up until my body felt clean,
but I didn't,
because thinking of you made me sad
and I didn't buy anything.
I left the store and said to myself,
"I'm sorry I'm like this,"
and months passed reading poetry
and taking baths that got cold before I noticed
because I kept dissociating to feel
hopeful about my life.
Now I'm studying German on Duolingo
and I can't help but think
if I learn enough of it
we can go there together next time
but at this point,
you're probably planning
for that trip to Scotland, which
we used to joke about having
on our honeymoon which I know
was absolutely a joke
because I had only just met you
but it was also kind of real
because it felt possible,
even then, and
I felt that the first time I saw you
in your fake FBI jacket and shades.

———

Someday, after another Pope is coronated and
I have a new degree and

you are rich and
your son is at college and
my daughter is writing intelligible words,
I will maybe think of you
without imploding
or dissociating
down a dark rabbit hole.

The only thing left in 100 years will be love.
Everything else leaves.
Dogs die.
Parents die.
Lovers die.
You will die and I will die.
The world blacks out,
changes clothes,
an entirely new wardrobe.
The only eternal experience is love.
Love transcends time.
Love transcends lovers.
It's only cliché if you don't know what it means.

I didn't know what I wanted,
but I knew what I didn't want.
I didn't want a smiling therapist,
a whole personality formed from textbooks,
gatekeepers, APA papers,
Benzos and beta blockers.
Influencers regurgitating
self-help books through memes.
I didn't want love instructions,
fast-fashion dating,
law of assumption acolytes,
paint by number spiritual quests.
I craved a new world,
a new geography,
the Azores, the Highlands,
limestone, rain.
I wanted a flood of watery gold light,
to wash away my discontent.
Time was dead, the gods were sterile.
We were all mad,
madness was compartmentalized,
demonetized, demoralized,
madness was reprimanded,
creativity was cybernated,
spirituality was commodified,
love was merchandised.
We were shamans searching for fans,
tadpoles searching for land,
kittens demanding to be fed.
We were dreamers,
distracting, numbing, wilting,
raging, stretching, emerging.
We moved away to perceive what we had,
we moved away to come back to ourselves.

God has no face,
no voice,
no body.
God is just trees, rocks, water,
dirt, light, space,
cells, stars.
Inside and outside of form.
In your eyes and mine.

I took the red pill.
Divorce. Freedom. Hope.
Singing songs to my little girl at bed time.
Holding her hand while she slept.
A hot shower in the middle of the night.
Eating ice cream in bed.
Matcha and a walk in the rain.
No more fear.
No more choking.
No more hating things I loved.
Sometimes aloneness is a gift.

Idea: bathtubs soft as marshmallows so you can sit in them for hours without hurting your butt

Idea: an adult coloring book but for your taxes

Idea: a sensory deprivation tank but it's just your bathtub in the dark

Idea: men who have healed their inner childhood trauma and aren't afraid to dance

Idea: love, but it's a two-way street, with no beginning, no middle, and no end

You don't have to be sad right now.
Put down your phone and smell a flower.
When you take a bath,
dip your head underwater and
blow all the negative thoughts out.
They'll be trapped in bubbles and float out the door.
Try not to carry resentment with you
along with trash and old newspapers.
Bitterness will destroy you.
Smash eggs on a redneck's truck.
Beat the shit out of a snowman.
Release.
Water is very good for you.
You should drink at least 1,024 tablespoons of water a day.
Keep your toes flexible and eat plants.
Try not to be a terrible human,
unless you're too terrible to know better.
Don't trust anybody who doesn't like to dance.
And damn the people who get in your way
when you're trying to stop in the middle of the road
to take a picture of a barn.
Burn a few bridges and
take out a few trash cans.
If you ever feel like you haven't
accomplished enough in your life,
remember you're just stardust and will
be forgotten before a century has passed.
Move to the middle of nowhere and
find someone to explore like a map.
Grow old with them and wake up
every morning grateful they're not dead yet.
And if there is no one, find a dog.
They are better.
Life is horrifying.
You just have to accept that
and then it will be great.

Is this joy?
Planning nothing, hiding
in music, in baths, in coffee, indisposed,
Saudade, the melancholy,
Was it inherited from generations lost?
I would leave,
the military brat disappearing act,
"how are you doing, single mom, no man, no family
around..."
"The price you pay for freedom",
people would say.
"But family is everything",
people would say.
You cannot make your life the way you want
with all these people pushing on your backside.
The divorces and fragments of roots,
a desiderium from the Azores to California.
I constructed a 360-degree picture.
Who and what formed me.
The music, food, photographs, memories,
good friends, fake friends, soulmates, fuckboys,
a constellation of cracks in my china,
the ghosts that pulled feelings through my ribs
and spilled them over the sky
with pollen, dust, rays of light, a deep breath.
Turn the page.

The sun rose in my cluttered apartment.
Books, dirty dishes, flowers,
tea leaves, empty cups, plants.
By the window, a faint rainbow from a crystal.
Barefoot, I smooshed a toe in the red.
Somewhere, beneath the floor,
a child threw a ball at the ceiling.
Thump.
"This is where I'll heal," I thought. "Where I'll learn to love myself."
I opened a letter. Another bill.
Thump.
"This is all there is." Endless separations, check lists, tasks,
books, tea leaves, thoughts, hopes, sulky silences…
until we love ourselves.
Thump.

Buy flowers, buy wine, buy sun fucked tea,
self-care with Al-Anon workbooks,
King Arthur's sword was the golden key,
memory faint with ecstasy highs.
Could I push a button in my mind,
feel that violent serenity again?
Trolling the grandeur of museum exhibits,
trolling the emeralds and pearls in your eyes.
I'd write about sex to make up for celibacy,
a string of dates with plastic dicks.
Old pictures in my head, fading.
It's not just men who get consumed by sex.
My whole day I think about it.
With you. What would that be like?
A graceful gesture, a solo elevator ride,
inaudible shame, the same mental game.
My signature longing.
The fingernail moon milking the sky,
the last bits of tapering sun,
burnt like cigarette butts.
I could hear time move.
Nothing made me do anything now.
I just did things and let things be done.

Silence.
Death is quiet.
All sunsets end.
The dark is where we grow.
We have reached the coda in a long arrangement of verse.
Listen.
Rest.
Heal.
Dissect your blind spots at the table.
Your heart is searching only to find itself.

———

Noise.
All sunrises begin.
The light is where we engage.
We have reached the crescendo in a long arrangement of
verse.
Communicate.
Change.
Play.
Integrate your shadow at the table.
Your mind is searching only to release itself.

Playlist for this book–

会いたい

Birdsong
Regina Spektor

Time To Say Goodbye
Sarah Brightman, Andrea Bocelli

Do I Ever Cross Your Mind
Chet Atkins and Dolly Parton

Angela (Theme from Taxi)
Bob James

September Song
Agnes Obel

Ruby
Ali Farka Touré, Toumani Diabaté

The Single Petal Of A Rose
Duke Ellington

Strings That Tie to You
Yellow Ostrich

Heart of Gold
Crosby, Nash, Young

Isn't It a Pity
Nina Simone

Ride Into The Sun— "1969"/2014 Mix
The Velvet Underground

Untitled Melancholy Song— Demo
Elliott Smith

The Sound of Silence—Acoustic Version
Simon & Garfunkel

is it better to speak or to die?
Cesourius

Be My Friend
Free

Odi et Amo
Jóhann Jóhannsson

Where or When
Benny Goodman Trio

When I Die
Beirut

The Night We Met (feat. Phoebe Bridgers)
Lord Huron, Phoebe Bridgers

Alone in Kyoto
Air

Golden Brown
The Stranglers

I Know (feat. Fiona Apple)
King Princess, Fiona Apple

Long Long Time
Linda Ronstadt

Mary
Big Thief

Deep In Love
Bonny Light Horseman

Nos Quedamos Solitos
ROSALÍA

Believe
Okay Kaya

The Sun
Mirah

Turiya & Ramakrishna
Alice Coltrane

Poems and
illustrations by:

Claudia Turner

Other books by Claudia Turner:

Notes on a Hospitalized Pregnant Woman

Claudia Turner is an artist, writer, photographer, and mom. Her first book, *Notes on a Hospitalized Pregnant Woman,* was a memoir about her experience with preeclampsia and being swept away to a distant hospital for 2.5 months of bed rest. In this new collection of poetry, Claudia delves into the subconscious with a mix of feelings, humor, the phases of heartbreak and grief, and what it is to create an authentic life. To learn more about Claudia and her other projects, including oracle cards about Victorian slang, go to www.claudiaturner.com.

ISBN: 979-8-8622-3542-5

Art, Illustrations by Claudia Turner

www.claudiaturner.com

Milton Keynes UK
Ingram Content Group UK Ltd.
UKHW051818291123
433461UK00004B/72